Author: Hildreth York
Editor: Matthew Koumis
Graphic Design: Rachael Dadd & MK
Reprographics: Ermanno Beverari
Printed in Italy by Grafiche AZ

© Telos Art Publishing 2003

Telos Art Publishing
PO Box 125, Winchester
SO23 7UJ England
t: +44 (0) 1962 864546
f: +44 (0) 1962 864727
e: editorial@telos.net
e: sales@telos.net
w: www.telos.net

ISBN 1 902015 41 X (softback)
ISBN 1 902015 58 4 (hardback)

A CIP catalogue record for this book is
available from The British Library

Notes

All dimensions are shown in metric and
imperial, height x width x depth.
All work is in private collections unless
otherwise stated.

Photo Credits

Jason Harris, Doug Koch, E.G. Schempf,
Jon Blumb, Kelly Mills

Artist's Acknowledgments

I dedicate this book to my parents, Tony
and Dianne Lordi. Their ongoing love of
learning inspires me.

I am sincerely grateful to Hildreth York
for her insightful and thoughtful essay,
and to Ilze Aviks for her generous
comments. Thank you to Matthew
Koumis and Jason Harris for guidance
and creative problem solving.

I would also like to thank my sisters,
Barbara and Karen, for their sustaining
belief in my work, and finally, my
husband Dennis and children Sara and
David, for their continual support of
good humor and love.

Publisher's Acknowledgements

Thanks to Freya, Simone, Stefania,
Ian Chalmers, Paul Richardson,
John Denison, Sue Atkinson, Erin Prues
and Kristina Detwiller.

Author's Bibliography

Arguelles, Jose A.
'Art as Internal Technology,' pp.174-185
Esthetics Contemporary (ed. Richard
Kostelanetz)
Buffalo NY: Prometheus Books, 1978

Arnheim, Rudolf
Visual Thinking
Berkeley, CA: University of California Press, 1969

Barber, Elizabeth Wayland
Women's Work: The First 20,000 Years
New York: W. W. Norton & Company, 1995

Dissanayake, Ellen
What is Art For?
Seattle WA: University of Washington Press,
1988

Fricke, Michele
'Susan Lordi Marker: Explorations in Cloth'
Surface Design Journal 23:2, Winter 1999

Gardner, Howard
The Arts and Human Development
New York: John Wiley & Sons, 1973

Jeneiro, Jan
'Text in Textiles,' *Fiberarts* 18:1, 1991, pp. 28-31

Art Textiles of the World: USA vol. 1
(ed.) Matthew Koumis
Winchester, England: Telos Art Publishing, 2000

Marker, Susan Lordi
'Resonant Voices: A Master's Thesis'
Surface Design Journal 18:3, Spring 1994

portfolio collection
Susan Lordi Marker

TELOS

Contents

Untapped
1993
cotton, wood,
rope, thread
30 x 33 x 8in (78 x 86 x 21cm)

page 1 & 48:
Rust Print Study
2002
cotton, iron oxide
10 x 10in (26 x 26cm)

Foreword

The *Soulskin* series is a wonderful place to begin talking about the emotional power of Susan Lordi Marker's textile art. The subject matter is our connection with our past and what we learn about ourselves when we examine our own history. If you possess heirlooms passed from generation to generation you know the almost urgent need to preserve and protect them. These mementos are not 'everyday' objects – they are 'charged', surrounded by an emotional space.

Marker displays images of clothing directly, straightforwardly, as the actual *objects* they are. But these images, starchy, flat, ghostly white, also become iconic as they float in a rich field of text, stitches, and pattern. Perhaps this white gown was used in a special family ritual? Clearly, the artist believes that cloth can convey potent emotional and intellectual associations.

Marker's richly worked textiles have 'presence' and seem to have absorbed past lives and places. Images and text are alternatively submerged and revealed in fragile transparencies suggesting half-finished conversations and narratives. Her more recent landscape-inspired work conveys the shifting, elusive patterns underlying nature, recorded from attentive observation. The astonishingly detailed surfaces seduce the viewer into further contemplating the layers of meaning.

The sensory impact of Marker's textiles goes beyond good aesthetics. The evidence of time and commitment is palpable. When cloque is used, effecting a fascinating surface relief, the viewer must share some feeling of the intense patience and vision involved in building cloth so architecturally from micro to macro.

The process is not gratuitous or an ironic display of obsession; Marker has said that she loves working with cloth and allowing the materials to speak.

Such presence and emotional impact in an artwork is perhaps more meaningful than ever, as pervasive electronic media in the popular culture competes for our sensory attention. The art 'object' has undergone theoretical reconsideration as emblematic of the commerce of art or exclusionary museum politics. Even in the ancient world, Plato warned against the imitative nature of art, which distances it from true 'reality'. In the 1930s, Walter Benjamin feared that the age of mechanical reproduction and mass culture was signaling the loss of 'aura', the unique, primal quality of an artwork.

Contemporary artists have the freedom to place their work in new contexts. Listening to Susan Lordi Marker talk about her work reminds us that she thinks deeply about content, and is aware of the need for connectivity. Her intellectual involvement cannot be separated from the making. By virtue of the joyous, even devotional process, the subject matter here also becomes *cloth*, the *making* of cloth, and communal memory. What an appropriate approach to convey the ritual nature of creating and a belief in the potency of objects. It reminds us that the art can be surrounded by an emotional space.

Ilze Aviks

Artist and writer
Durango, Colorado
2002

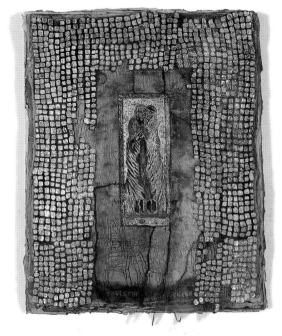

Soulskin: Forgiveness
1994
linen, silk, paper, gold leaf,
thread, pigment, dye
27 x 22 x 1in (71 x 58 x 3cm)

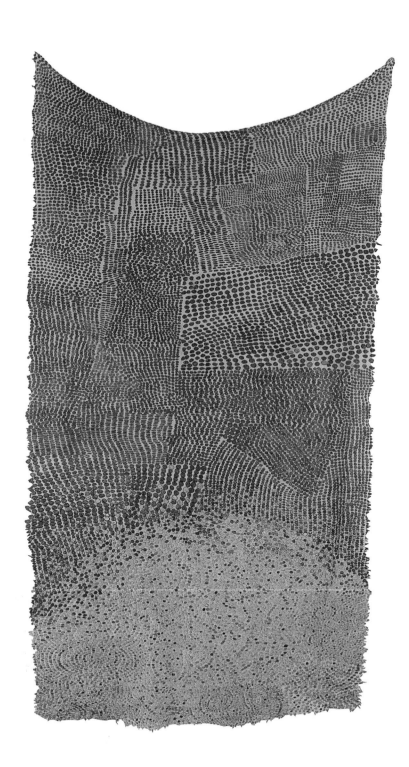

Soulskin: Seeding the Prairie
1999
(detail on page 29)
nylon, iron, copper, pigment
76 x 41 x 3in (197 x 107 x 8cm)

Concerning the land

Somewhere in Missouri is a stretch of prairie owned by Susan Lordi Marker. There the artist is carefully and lovingly restoring the prairie grasses that once were the glory of the plains. With her passion for nature and natural forms, Marker is assisting in the rebirth of a complex ecosystem that we are finally beginning to understand and value. This land, where the artist spends time whenever possible, is not only a place to center her mind and soul, but a metaphor for the theme of continuity, regeneration and the cycle of life at the core of all her work.

Evidence: Preservation and process

"Who or what is the true 'keeper' of the records?"
    Susan Lordi Marker [1]

We know who we are and who we were because the memories have been kept, in song and poem, epic and myth, sung and scribed through the centuries by generations of those who believed we are best led toward the future by honoring and learning from our ancestors. Yet many of us born in the United States have genealogies as brief as our young country is old, and often not even that. For us, family histories cannot penetrate the curtain drawn across our past, barely parted by tales of parents, grandparents and those before them who wearily descended from ships onto this promised land, carrying their few most precious belongings.

Many who came in the waves of immigration from Europe and elsewhere, grateful to escape poverty, famine and discrimination, often found that their children sought to escape the traditions and cultures that had shaped their parents. The myth of America as the great melting pot has given rise to an immense body of literature and films, in which members of a younger generation examine and attempt to reconcile identities hovering between past and present.

Susan Lordi Marker has explored the many layers of her personal and family heritage through her art in textile and fiber. Affection for those who were the bearers of the family's Sicilian and Italian heritage was part of her childhood and has shaped her adulthood. However, the intense, and often poignant works of the artist's last fifteen years could not have been anticipated by her first career.

Her undergraduate B.S. concentration was in Environmental Design, and a number of years were spent designing interior environments for the restaurant industry. College included several art courses, and art history was a discipline Marker loved. She continued taking graduate art courses, primarily drawing and painting, while working. A major shift in direction occurred when Marker lost her job at the time she was pregnant with her first child. She continued studying art and as her children started school she began taking textile courses at the University of Kansas. In her mid-30s, Marker started graduate studies there with a scholarship and a teaching assistantship.

It all came together in her graduate years – her travels, her long time interest in other cultures, her intellectual curiosity, her well-developed technical skills and the self- discipline demanded by roles as wife, mother, student and artist.

page 12:
Old Stories
(detail)
1991
silk, rayon, dye,
pigment, thread, wood.
72 x 18 x 6in (188 x 47 x 16cm)

page 13:
Lost Dialect
(detail)
silk, thread, dye
72 x 18 x 6in
(188 x 47 x 16cm)

In interviewing Marker, she counted among her influences her mother's love of history and travel, and the many hours spent in museums, looking at the artifacts of other periods and cultures. Medieval paintings and Moorish tiles are still recalled with visible pleasure. Travel to Italy and Sicily clearly fed the artist's deep need to keep alive in some unique way the spiritual identity that she carried from her forebears. To do this, Marker researched and brought together a family history, interviewing those of the older generation who could provide not only information, stories and proverbs, but actual material fragments of the past in the form of cloth and articles of clothing.

"Tangible objects which are physical evidence of people's lives are also metaphors for their life experience and traditions." [2]

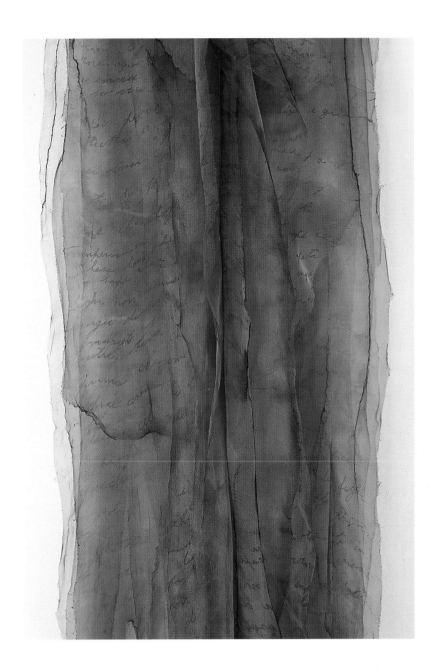

Susan Lordi Marker's great grandmother was a weaver from a village in Sicily, who brought to America a number of garments and pieces of cloth. Some were handed down to the artist from her great grandmother's hope chest, where they had been 'kept for good,' i.e., never used and never worn. Some of them have been incorporated into the artist's work, carrying with them, intact, the power of generations of women's work. A marvelous nineteenth century quotation expresses this:

"White linen is the paper of [housewives], which must be on hand in great, well-ordered layers, and therein they write their entire philosophy of life, their woes and their joys."[3]

The work of a woman's hands was a mark of her accomplishments and her value. Spinning and weaving from the earliest times were more often than not an economic necessity. That they found their way into some of the most profound myths and tales of several cultures is not surprising. The Moirai of ancient Greece, three goddesses who were collectively Fate, were envisioned as spinners, who spun, allotted, and ultimately cut the thread of life. In Homer's *Odyssey*, Penelope, an exemplar of virtue and fidelity, wove by day, and unraveled her work every night, to hold off the suitors during Ulysses' prolonged absence. In legends, folk- and fairytales, spinning, weaving, and the resultant cloth are often magical and protective. The textile arts have even more ancient power and significance, not only as metaphors for the worth of women but for woman's unique role in bringing life into the world.

Evidence and interpretation suggest that textiles may well have carried such beliefs from deepest antiquity to more modern folk traditions. [4]

Susan Lordi Marker knows that the textile artifacts created by her family are the vehicles of continuity and the carriers of life. Her work references this in a number of ways, earlier on through the use of actual pieces or duplicates made by the artist, and increasingly in later work through symbolic materials and abstract forms. It is not surprising that a number of her titles *They Left Their Land* and *Old Stories* confirm the content of some works, even when the piece is entirely non-objective.

Experimentation and early work

"Making art, with textiles as my chosen medium, aligns me with those for whom process and materials play an important role in motivating concept and form. The intimacy I seek in my pieces depends on engaging or seducing the viewer with transformation of surfaces and materials. The versatility of textiles allows this to happen in unexpected and unique ways...the process, as well as the materials, reveal – and I try to listen." Susan Lordi Marker [5]

Marker's handmade 'book' of experiments is especially intriguing: Swatches of material, images of various sorts, are stitched together as if they were fragments of dreams, complex and multi-layered as dreams are. The pieces in this book sometimes precede, but often accompany the development of ongoing work. In this gathering of samples are ideas and images that will occur in finished work. Even the most spontaneous-seeming of Marker's early and later pieces may have undergone arduous rehearsal, possibly in more than one medium. The book of experiments is, in a very real sense, the artist's visual diary.

On one of the 'pages' a figure suddenly springs upward, the image of a joyful young boy, arms flung up, his body patterned with green and yellow, except for the hands which are wine red (1992). The background texture consists of plant motifs, frequently seen in the artist's textiles. Susan Lordi Marker has talked about her love of natural forms, of the "fibrousness" of prairie grasses. The variations in such forms are a visual counterpoint to the regularity of woven textile structure.

Book of Experiments
1992-97

The repertoire of photoscreened images of her children, of plant forms, of vegetal motifs and textures are precursors of content seen again in later work. The samples reveal the artist's investigation of a variety of techniques and materials as well as the use of mixed media. Marker's experiments with resists, with the layering of colors, with photoscreened and manipulated imagery are all here, interleaved in this gathering of possibilities. On some pages of the handmade book bits of fragmentary text float up from deep color. Text in Marker's early work is screened, but later is actually etched into the fabric.

A small early work, *Study: Chrysalid* (1992) points to future possibilities. It consists of a nude female, curled into a fetal position, on a dark field of pale grass texture, with a border on one side of pomegranate forms in warm orange tones. Such brave and surprising color shifts and unexpected conjunctions of imagery enliven this and other works. The image of the pomegranate with its mythic history is seen in other examples. An ancient symbol of fertility and regeneration, the fruit is associated with the tale of Persephone, the daughter of Demeter, the goddess of agricultural fertility. Seized by Hades, the god of the underworld, Persephone was forced to spend half of each year on earth and half in Hades' domain after eating pomegranate seeds. In the myth's tradition, Persephone is kept safe by her mother in Sicily, their island – and, coincidentally, the land of Marker's ancestors.

Crucial to the evolution of Susan Lordi Marker's art was her participation in one of the early workshops given in this country by Joy Boutrup, who came to the Kansas City Art Institute in May 1993, at the invitation of Jason Pollen. Processes previously for industrial use were demonstrated for their applicability to studio textile arts. These 'new tools' were disseminated over the next few years at several workshops including those at Penland and the Surface Design Association Conference. The physical layering and fusing of cloth, the joining and manipulation of surfaces through stitching and lye crimping (cloqué), and the use of chemical burn-out (dévoré), provided the technical means for Marker to explore and enrich her palimpsests of forms and layered membranes of cloth. The amazing ability of cloth to survive in spite of its vulnerability became a metaphor for life itself, and for the history that the artist compiled of her family. It is important to note, however, that Marker's work is never specifically narrative or historical in content or form.

By the early 1990s, Susan Lordi Marker's work was being exhibited and receiving awards, and in 1993 and 1994 she had three one-person exhibitions. It became clear that qualities in her art resonated with jurors and viewers. The work of the early '90s is already highly skilled, suggesting that Marker's several years in design, although not her ultimate choice, nurtured her esthetic sophistication.

The early 1990s: Work of the heart

Damiana's Cloth (1991) is composed of layers of cloth with raw edges. The surface appears abraded by time and usage. Illegible text floats within the layers, becoming more visible on the reverse of a section that has been ripped open and turned back.

Typical of almost all of Marker's exhibited work is her willingness to let cloth sag, pulled down by its own weight, but securely (and invisibly) suspended. Her work has always been about the essence of cloth, its properties and its propensities and to this end great effort is expended on creating appropriate installation hardware to achieve the artist's intentions.

Part of the attraction of Marker's work is the viewer's kinesthetic familiarity with the behavior of cloth, even the primitive honesty of raw edges. The tearing of cloth, the sense of age, evoke the universal past of women, its traditional makers. *Damiana's Cloth*, while intimate, resonates with something very ancient and archaic, a deeper wellspring of archetypes awakened in the creative process, and perhaps more rooted in ancestral need than we imagine. Damiana was the artist's Sicilian great grandmother. We do not necessarily need to know that, but it informs us of the emotional and personal resources that Marker draws upon. The 'pocket' into the interior of the piece is a motif in other works as well, as if art, like life, has secret and hidden places.

right:
Damiana's Cloth
1991
rayon, silk, thread
22 x 25 x 3in (58 x 65 x 7cm)

page 16:
Study: Chrysalid
1992
cotton, pigment, photo transfer
9 x 9in (23 x 23cm)

Manifesto
1993
cotton, nylon, thread, dye
65 x 65 x 5in (169 x 169 x 13cm)

Other works of this period explore themes evocative of the artist's history: *Old Stories* (1991), *Sympathetic Resonance* (1992), and *Passageways* (1993). Somewhat more concrete in its allusions are works such as *Manifesto* (1993). Here, pockets of sheer cloth are layered and printed with fragments of actual ship manifestos and details of clothing, the records and artifacts of arriving immigrants, visually whispering information about their bearers, stitched together as all histories are, and subtly dyed to the tones of aged cloth.

Also of this period of Marker's work is *Chrysalid* (1993), consisting of bound and wrapped bundles contained within a framing of cloth and paper layered and pieced together. Barely legible text is visible within each bundle. Should the viewer react to these as if each bound form might someday emerge from its chrysalis to reveal its concealed information? Or should these silent entities be regarded as eternally sealed, small mummified remnants of a past that is never to be fully understood? The seductive ambiguity intensifies the mystery of Marker's work.

Written language, often integral in Marker's work, functions as a visual form, denying the viewer full awareness of meaning. The words elude us, and thereby haunt us, murmuring subliminally. The use of image and text together have a long chronology – the hieroglyphs in Egyptian art, the royal monuments of ancient Mesopotamia with cuneiform inscriptions carved into the figurative narratives. Every literate culture has brought word and image together – the richly illustrated books of Medieval and Renaissance Europe are certainly familiar. Marker's use of text functions as symbol rather than specific legible reference. Howard Gardner characterizes this capability of the creative individual: "... [the artist's] actions, perceptions, and feelings are directed toward symbols, elements that have become imbued with a referential significance, that stand for his feelings, experiences, ideas, knowledge, objects and desires, that exemplify qualities and properties of importance to him. Only the symbol user can leave the world of his direct experience and go on to create new worlds in his imagination, or to discover such worlds by 'reading' the symbols of others." [6]

"It is not so important that the words are able to be read; rather, that they connote communication beyond the written word."

Susan Lordi Marker [7]

Chrysalid
1993
mixed media
24 x 32 x 9in (63 x 84 x 23cm)

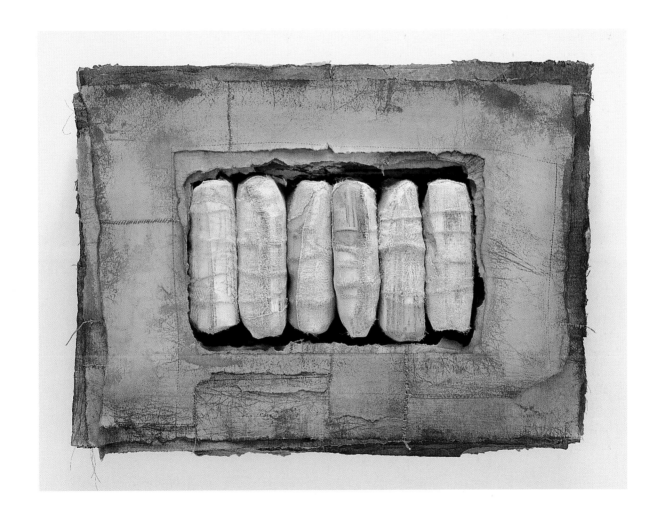

Excavation: Soulskin # 11

1997

linen blend, thread, dye, pigment

66 x 34in (172 x 89cm)

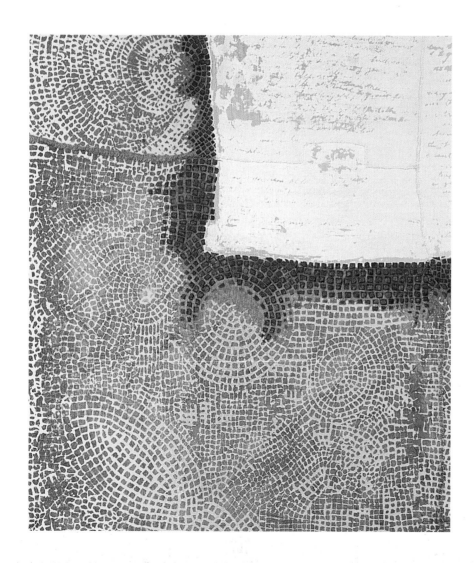

Work of the late 1990s: Further abstraction, deepening strata

By 1997 the years of experimentation and the artist's continued work with the 'new tools' led to a new series of works still referencing her family heritage, but moving toward more fully abstract form-making. The sample book and other small pieces show expert and ingenious use of dévoré and cloqué. Layers of textile increasingly manipulate variations in transparency and texture. Gold and metal leaf appear on some pieces. Raw edges of cloth confirm the essential nature of woven textile.

One of this writer's favorites among the smaller works of this intermediate period is *Milagros* (1997). Marker here pushes the potentials of dévoré, cloqué and relief. A central panel of linen/poly is embellished with irregular small raised silver shapes.

left:

Milagros
1997
linen blend, silver leaf
12 x 18in (32 x 47cm)

This is framed by a border of patterned black spirals on a sheer poly ground left after burning out the linen. The spirals will be seen on a number of pieces over the years. They have the timelessness of natural forms and the irregularities of the artist's working hand. The title obviously refers to the small silver votive objects and amulets of Mexico, yet the shapes in this piece have no specific connotations. The scope of Marker's interest in material culture of the past, in the textiles, the objects, the relics of various civilizations, preserved fortuitously or purposefully, provides continual inspiration for her inventiveness.

Soulskin: Listening to Julia
1995
linen, silk, cotton, thread, dye
29 x 26in (76 x 68cm)

The series which the artist has titled *Excavations* co-exists in part with the *Soulskin* works of the mid- to late 1990s. The forms of garments are prominent elements in a few works; e.g. *Excavation Soulskin #11* (1997). The pale shape of a generic woman's dress floats on a ground of asymmetrical spirals on fabric made sheer through burning out.

Slightly earlier (1995) is the stunning, abstract *Soulskin: Listening to Julia*, which is dyed, stitched and dévoré. Barely visible text is etched into cloth that appears crackled and abraded by time. This work truly conveys the sense of a 'skin,' of a soul still hovering within the work. Julia was Marker's elderly aunt whose memories she recorded, and whose handwriting appears in this work.

Recent work: Touching the intangible

The series of work represented by *Seeding the Prairie* (1999), *Generations* (2000) and *Sun, Lake, Dragonfly* (2000) brings Marker's work into a new phase. Materials and techniques now fully exploit the use of dévoré and cloqué to create diaphanous textiles of impressively large size. The multiple layers of earlier work here give way to pieces that create dimensionality through mosaic-like patterns on sheer grounds. Copper and rust become dominant colors as Marker continues to investigate the use of metallics. These pieces, hung away from the wall (as are all of her works), cast patterned shadows that vary in tone and hue depending upon light and time of day. The temporal changes are as subtle as the movement of prairie grasses or the changing color of water as clouds pass. The spirals are here, the circling infinite metaphor for life in all its manifestations and the fragments of mosaic, fabric gem-stones left after burning out. The recent pieces shimmer with color: *Generations* brings together earth tones, gold, coppery metal and its patina. *Sun, Lake, Dragonfly* floats spirals of greens and blues, and suggests the iridescence of dragonfly wings on a transparent surface, a scrim revealing the landscape beyond. This is a work that seems to be made more of spirit than of cloth. Perhaps that is exactly what Susan Lordi Marker wished to achieve – the transmutation of the physical world into art.

Hildreth York

Hildreth York holds the Ph. D. in Art History from Columbia University (NYC) and is Professor Emerita, Rutgers The State University of New Jersey. She is currently President of the Board of Trustees of the Hunterdon Museum of Art in NJ.

1. Susan Lordi Marker in "Artists and Language" (catalog of an exhibition, Society for Contemporary Crafts, Pittsburgh PA 1993) p.12.
2. Susan Lordi Marker in "Artists and Language," p.12.
3. Gottfried Keller, "Der grune Heinrich" (1854) in Elizabeth Wayland Barber, *Women's Work: The First 20,000 Years* (New York: W. W. Norton & Company, 1995) p.232.
4. Barber, *passim*.
5. Susan Lordi Marker, "Resonant Voices: A Master's Thesis," in *Surface Design Journal* 18:3, Spring 1994, p.22.
6. Howard Gardner, *The Arts and Human Development* (New York: John Wiley & Sons, 1973) p. 87.
7. "Susan Lordi Marker," in *Art Textiles of the World: USA volume 1* (Winchester, England: Telos Art Publishing, 2000) p.88.

right:

Soulskin: Seeding the Prairie
1999
(detail, see page 9 for full caption)

page 30:
Generations I & II
2000
nylon, iron, pigment
132 x 32in (343 x 84cm)

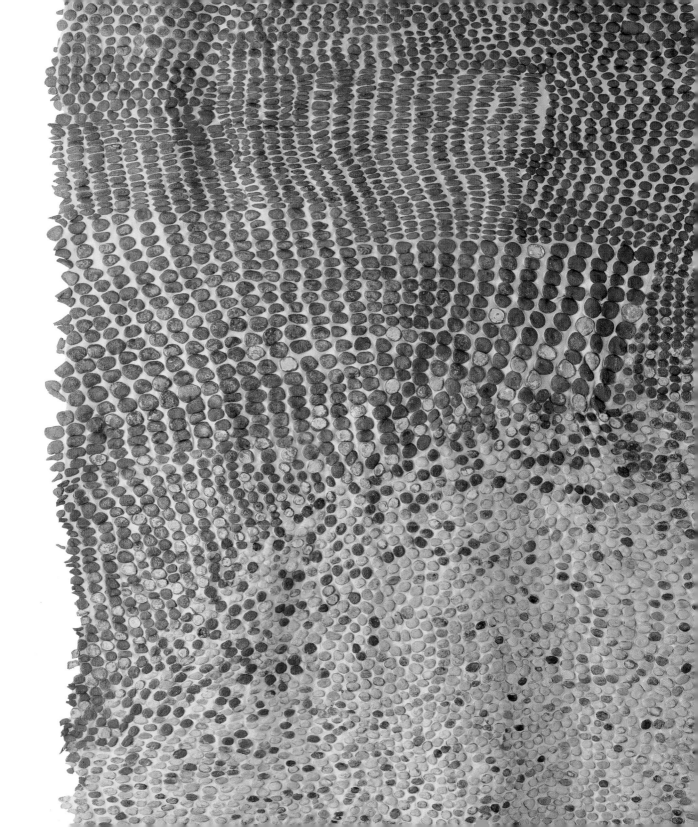

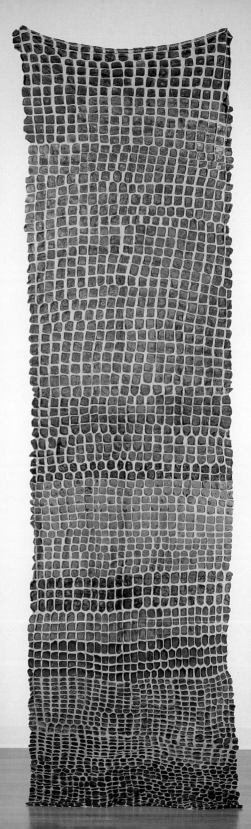

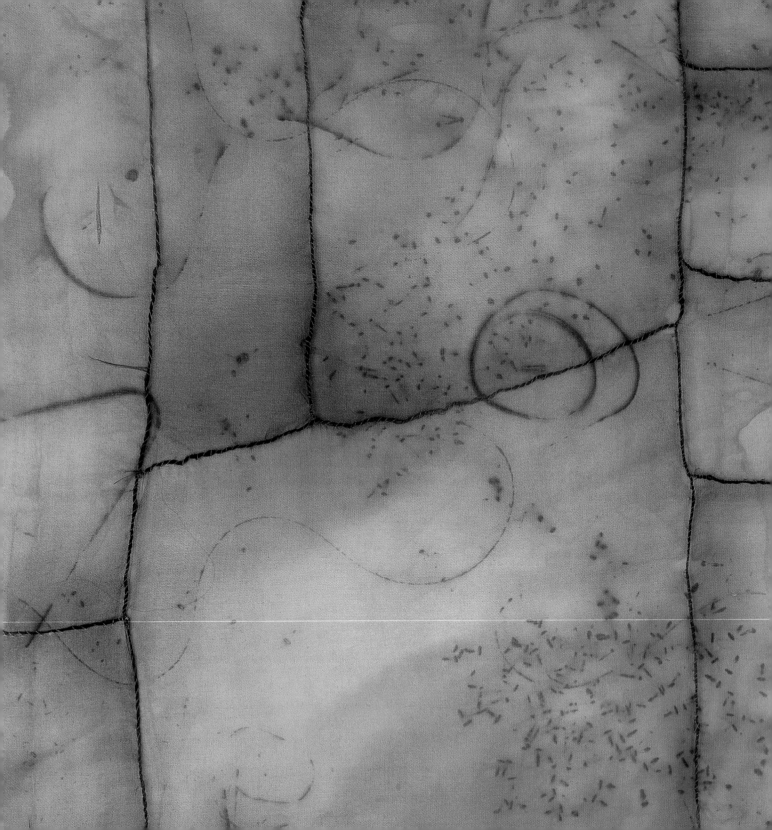

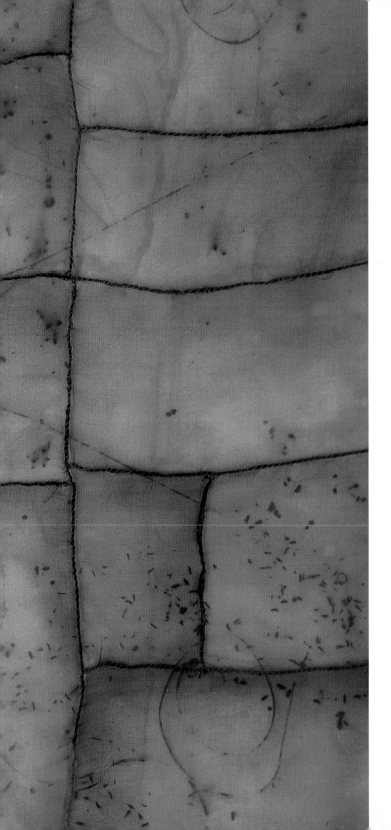

page 32:
explorations
1995 - 2002
cotton, linen, silk, pigment, dye,
thread, rust

page 33:
explorations
1995 - 2002
cotton, linen, silk, iron, gold leaf,
graphite, pigment, dye, thread

this page:
study for Beneath
(detail)
2002
cotton, silk, iron oxide, thread
22 x 26in (58 x 68cm)

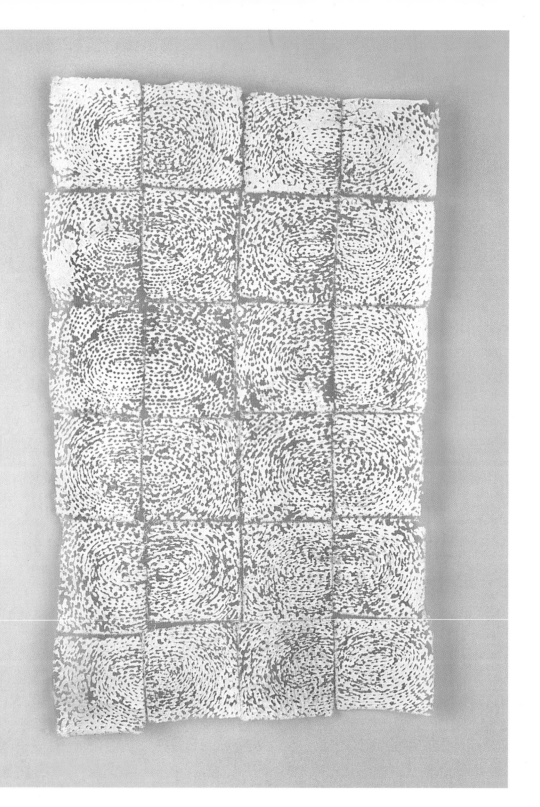

Quietly
2002
cotton, nylon
23 x 14in (60 x 37cm)

Soulskin: Sun, Lake, Dragonfly
(detail)
2000
linen blend, dye, pigment, gold leaf

Excavation: Soulskin # 10
1997
linen blend, thread, dye, pigment
30 x 47in (78 x 122cm)

Tree
1992
collage
11 x 8in (29 x 21cm)

Biography

Born

1954,   Beaver Falls, Pennsylvania

Education and Awards

1976   Bachelor of Science, cum laude, University of Missouri, Columbia

1993   Master of Fine Arts, with honors, University of Kansas, Lawrence

1974   InterFuture Study Scholarship Award, University of Missouri, Columbia

1990, 91, 92, 93   Graduate Merit and Research Scholarship Awards, University of Kansas

1991   Second Prize, 'Fiberart International '91,' Pittsburgh, Pennsylvania

1992   Juror's Choice Award, 'Fiber Directions '92,' Wichita, Kansas

1993   Juror's Choice Award, 'International '93,' Pittsburgh, Pennsylvania

1994   International Judges Award, 'International Textile Design Contest,' Tokyo, Japan

1998   Best of Show Award, 'Muse of the Millennium,' Seattle, Washington

Selected Solo and Group Exhibitions

2003   'Generations/Transformations: American Fiber Art,' American Textile History
                           Museum, Lowell, Massachusetts

2003   'The Metal Show', virtual gallery show, FiberScene

2001   'A Legacy of Inspiration', Penland Gallery, Penland, North Carolina

2001   'Textiles: Contemplative Language', Southern Illinois University, Edwardsville, Illinois

2000   'Material Evidence', Reed Whipple Center, Las Vegas, Nevada (tour)

2000   'Measure for Measure', H&R Block Artspace, Kansas City, Missouri

1999	'Past as Prologue,' The Society for Contemporary Crafts, Pittsburgh, Pennsylvania
1999	'Beneath the Surface,' Center of Contemporary Crafts (COCA), St. Louis, Missouri
1999	'Rising to the Surface,' Southern Oregon University, Ashland, Oregon
1998	'Muse of the Millennium: Emerging Trends in Fiber Art,' Nordic Heritage Museum, Seattle
1997	'Surface Tension: New Works in Textiles,' Center of Contemporary Arts (COCA), St. Louis, Missouri
1997	'Common Threads,' Art and Design Gallery, University of Kansas, Lawrence
1996-98	'Transcending the Surface,' Hunterdon Museum of Art, Clinton, New Jersey (tour)
1995-96	'Textile as Narrative / Ritual,' ARC Gallery, Chicago, Illinois (tour)
1995	'New Tools,' Littman and White Gallery, Portland, Oregon
1994	'Susan Lordi Marker,' Appalachian Center for Crafts, Smithville, Tennessee (solo)
1994	'The International Textile Design Contest,' Tokyo, Japan
1993,94	'Chautauqua International for Fiber Art,' Dunkirk, New York
1993	'Artists and Language,' The Society for Contemporary Crafts, Pittsburgh, Pennsylvania
1993	'Susan Lordi Marker: Resonant Voices,' University of Kansas Art and Design Gallery (solo)
1993	'Unspoken Dialogues: Fiber Constructions by Susan Lordi Marker,' University of Kansas Regents Center, Overland Park (solo)
1991, 93	'Fiberart International Biennial,' Pittsburgh Center for the Arts, Pittsburgh, Pennsylvania
1991	'Perspectives From the Rim: The Next Generation,' University of Washington, Seattle, Washington

right:
Exploration
2000
cotton
6 x 6in (16 x 16cm)

Selected Publications and Reviews

2003	*Generations/Transformations: American Fiber Art*, exhibition catalogue, American Textile History Museum, Lowell, Massachusetts
2002	*Surface Design Journal* Vol. 26, No. 4, 'New Tools and the Legacy of Risk,' essay by Chad Alice Hagen
2001	*Surface Design Journal* Vol 25, No. 4, 'Textiles, a Contemplative Language,' essay by Laura Strand
	Surface Design Journal Vol. 25, No. 2, review by Patricia Malarcher
2000	*Art Textiles of the World: USA*, edited by Matthew Koumis, Telos Art Publishing
1999	*Surface Design Journal* Vol. 23, No. 2, 'Susan Lordi Marker: Explorations in Cloth,' essay by Michele Fricke
	Pittsburgh Post-Gazette, May 29, review by Mary Thomas
	Fiberarts Vol. 25, No. 4, review by Teresa Montgomery
1998	*American Craft*, Feb/March, review by Luanne Rimel
1997	*Fiberarts* Vol. 25, No. 2, Best of Show Award documentation
1995	*Fiberarts* Vol. 22, No. 3, New Works
	Fiberarts Vol. 21, No. 5, article by Gregg Johnson
1994	*Surface Design Journal* Vol. 18, No. 3, essay by Susan Lordi Marker
1993	*Fiberarts Vol. 20, No. 3*, 'Close to Home,' essay by Margo Mensing
	'Artists and Language', exhibition catalog, Society for Contemporary Crafts, Pittsburgh, Pennsylvania
	Pittsburgh Post-Gazette, February 5, review by Donald Miller

Professional

1998-01	Instructor, Fiber, Kansas City Art Institute
1995-98	Instructor, Design, Johnson County Community College
1993-95	Instructor, Textile Design, University of Kansas